THE KIDS & I

THE KIDS & I

LAGUAN RODGERS
Nicky So

For Buffalo, the box a baby giggled in, the dimensions a man can't shake.

In the course of action, he sat still, and it was then he truly contemplated the supreme function of the lungs. They weren't there necessarily to circulate air through the body, but to make sure he didn't take in too much all at once, as he scanned the whole of the village from the viewpoint of glasses with ever-changing lenses. Recalling. Treading. Being. Prismatic.

PART 1

USA (Unfinished States of Amer-)

The Kids and I

The kids and I aren't invited.
So we make reservations across the street.
Banging instruments on empty stomachs.
The cymbals force them to say, "Good morning."
When they blow smoke,
we unbutton our shirts and show off our scars.
The kids didn't come for massages.
I'm not one to be patronized.
We hear there's a mint in the cellar.
Don't skip town; we kind of need that combination.
When they blow smoke,
we comb out our hair and dance over the flakes.
"Why don't our quarters work at the bake sale?"
The kids and I need to know.
Long since digested the crumbs.
We trade aprons for dinner bells.
When they blow smoke,
we narrate with our hands and italicize subtitles.
The kids and I laugh more than them.
We pick flowers and revise our grandmothers' soups.
Scraps once left for bloodhounds.
We're fancy now and buy organic.

They're blowing smoke.
We're somewhere between reproach and
down power lines.
The kids and I are not relatives.
We happen to share premeditated slang.
One unified hoarse voice.
That bats its eyes at the beautiful yellow moon.
When they snort smoke at us,
we never blow it back.
That would be rude.
The sunshine is our friend.
Yes, Lord—sweet keeper of our souls.
Yes, Lord.
We are your failing workers.
The kids and I.

The State of Black Souls

Where a crowd can form,
so can a forceful movement.
If a tongue curses and belittles,
it can uplift and sweetly instruct.
In the armpits of passion
there can be monologues of enlightenment.
For every sneaker living for a glare,
let occasions to break new ground.
Come with heavy badges and knotted hair.
And may those anxious ears
hug the lost languages still treading the Atlantic,
waiting for rescue in a crowded shipyard.
That is nostalgia.
That is remembrance.
It is today's sleeping pulse.
And yet these souls are foreign to rest.
Another endless dawn
and twisted hymn,
sounding rather fine...
Looping down hallways immaculately painted,
masking birthmarks and cauterized files.

Faux Patriots (For Ahmaud Arbery)

Descending on a hill of peeling stamps and nervous leaves.
Confronted by a brood of flags swaying with the
morning.
The man whose cloth and post wave the highest says hello
as he checks the curbside mailbox.
I'm flashing past the house,
catch a glimpse of his hands.
Not a morsel of dirt—the wedding ring dull
and snug, forcing skin to bulge over and under its
golden rim.
That sweet flapping noise above and around me.
I can barely hear the birds, if there are any.
Careful not to step on the lawns on either side of me.
I've run down this street so many times,
but doing so with eyes closed deserves no prize.
A few steps further, eyes shut.
The usual parked cars taped along the curb.
Asking for a disaster, I know exactly where I am,
and how to mosey about.
Downright starving for equity.
The flapping of those allegiances burned into memory.

Home–the aroma of home.
Almost there, says the imagination,
crisscrossing in the blueness
of early light unfiltered. In this carved pocket of town,
I have no allies.
Not shaken about it. Just hungry.
Sweat camping on my brow.
The snapping of those materials within the breeze
hours after I'm gone.
Telling me all I need to know,
and a pace worth sustaining.
If that's allowed. In a neighborhood of first names.
Where I live softly.

Black Hole (Another Dimension)

Pitch dark. And save for the rhythmic sliding
of clocks all around the house,
I know I've collapsed through a black hole.
The black hole where a wolverine senses
my cologne sat on the clearance rack.
A black hole of clogged sewers.
The black hole of folks repeating themselves.
In that wide expanse I needed an interpreter.
The black hole of quick train rides.
An alternate hole where the trolley
flips off its carbonite track.
A black hole of fair weather marriages.
In that wide expanse when I rethought how
we ended things over breakfast. Or was it evening?
On a shelf in the black hole where I glue
pieces of late people's voices.
Then nosedive down the hall to play them on spotless
vinyl.
That black hole explaining dead customs
to expatriates who braid each other's hair.
A black hole releasing endless gusts.

The settling of that very hole
to a calm as May leaves its jacket.
It is quiet this morning,
or whatever time of day it is.
I've been staring at the sheen
left by the white light from the ceiling.
Almost ready to come down. And walk an obscure road.
A black hole. Instances when I am still.
In skin that matches the void.
Black.

Wedding Invitation

I'm new to this modest house
with all its water marks, hissing pipes and a
dingy microwave.
After a sweltering day, I find myself in the kitchen,
staring at magnets on the refrigerator
before I reach in for a popsicle or freezie.
A certain magnet I dig, specifically.
It's a dark charcoal one, a Seneca proverb
about thanking the ancestors for existing—
their low ends, rituals and swan songs,
yet those sorts of things I've added.
I turn out the lights in an attempt to read the words,
the purple and teal letters arm-locked together
behind coarse shadows.
The whole scene really just a sheet of darkness
mocking my eyes for relying on any slice of natural light.
This is all quite odd I think to myself
with my back to the moon.
Cylindrical bulb over the sink pops on—jars, cabinets
and Keurig shimmering white now.
And if it weren't for a cheap magnet—
a rubbery cutout of fruits—

sliding down the icebox's face onto the tile,
I would've missed the wedding invitation.
Someone in this household is invited to a ceremony in
South Carolina on what once was a thriving plantation.
A few months out, the guest has yet to RSVP.
I could research this particular estate's history,
but I'm certain it was cotton not rice, sugar or morale.
Its towering columns and wide porches perfect for
rocking chairs and tall Old Testament tales.
The bride and groom know nothing beyond it being
prime real estate and suitable for Cinderella-themed
entrances, a frayed jumper cable to Antebellum,
an uncontested way of life and its clattering of
lemonade glasses.
Would guests walk the grounds and smell soil
like early morning coffee?
Would they hear the wailing over the breeze?
I'm standing here, imagining all this deciding whether to
tell my grandmother there are people exchanging vows
in the very fields she bolted from.
The other afternoon someone in my new home
chastised my pessimism and dissection of rainbows.
I open the freezer door. Reach in and grab a freezie.
Then a popsicle with chunky ice crystals at its base.
I wonder if my dead ancestors would've ever guessed
such a place could be happy.
I thank them for being. Turn the lights out.
Sweating just a bit—a few months early.
I may just go. I might.

Dead Barbie

Rain is a tolerable mist.
It somewhat poured the night before,
which left mini lakes sitting in random folds
of the intersection. I park under some maple and
walk a block to where I know she was when I turned.
Prone on the wet street without a thread of clothes
save for hot pink bracelets still on her skinny wrists,
and one leg warmer sagging down a plastic calf.
Never seen a lifeless woman up close.
Kick her over with my shoe, then regret my own indecency.
Ice blue eyes wide open looking back at me.
She doesn't blink or flick aside the strands of horse hair
stuck to those blushing cheeks.
I want to return with suitable attire
and give this young white chick a proper burial.
Cars whiz by. She rolls on like a barrel at sea.
Where's the spires and comforting verses
when I need them? No one stops or turns a head...
Just me and the soundtrack of rubber.
Reach in my shallow pocket,
all I find is a piece of Kleenex.
Drape it over her, mumble something like a prayer

that I remember from bedside.
She still lets the hair plaster to her bruised face.
But those eyes—eyes the color of Viking lore—
they still see me beneath the soaked tissue.
Her real assailant still out there.
White pulp covering her skin. Absorbing it almost.
She can't take her eyes off me—alive and murdered.
On the right side of town.

Riots Then Rain & Maybe Love (June 2020)

I heard the rolling thunder
and flashes of lightning just came by.
You say you wish I could come crosstown
and be with you.
We could listen to the booms and
jump at the surges of light with all the lamps off
in your room.
Do you hear sirens and wheels
charging to meet some catastrophe
brewing in the roads? On my side I can,
even the voices that try not to be loud.
Our city is ablaze, and we are separated.
On two ends of the dented compass.
Two nerds. Calm about who we are.
Waning balls of gas that can't wait
to collide and laugh until morning arrives
and turns it all back to shambles.
I'm awake. Wide awake purely for you.
Let's remember the fire and water

after they say normalcy has returned.
Next month...Next year...Or sometime.
We can't trust their historians.
They'll lie to people who were there
and pound their fists on the oak table.
The table shakes. Everything's trembling
like china in nervous hands.
And Zeus snores away
clenching what's left of a broken sky.

Bangladesh Girl

Call it a narrow-minded reason,
but a reason nonetheless.
I couldn't picture her boarding
a plane and sleeping all the way until the New World.
Her marble eyes just too wound up
to miss anything pretty and organic.
Like my daughter at that age,
she's missing some teeth—it's the time when they wear
frilly dresses and get stains the washer can't overcome.
"Take some kitty kitty," a lisp seeping through
holes in the screen
as she slightly shakes a cup over the feline.
Stray animals and people around here
are too prideful for warm gestures.
Rather odd never to see a mother or father or
wrinkled forebear pull her from the door.
Maybe they haven't heard about the shots hitting
windows early in the day?
Does she greet other strangers with a petite wave
and rising of bubble gum cheeks?
Her protectors have no idea what really goes on,
the problems we've revisited like sailor knots.

Do they know she could be hurt,
maimed by principles and codes?
Don't they adore her skin—the color of coffee
after creamer swirls around?
They placed her on the wrong coordinates,
which makes her hellos mean even more
to us who want to bid adieu and never return.
Her indigenous neighbors.
The smoke out of our clothes, at last.

Translations of a Journal 5.11.20

I didn't wish to rock the ship until I was cast into the waves underneath.

or

It was never my desire to cause commotion on deck. But something happened: My shipmates and I were cast aside without raft.

and/or

What the hell, man?! I'm gasping for a tiny pocket of air. You could care less because you're safe and full on a cruise.

Summer of Riots

A splash of watermelon
comes with a traveling mist.
The snap of nectarines
chiming along the tongue,
then the streets simmer in frenzy,
the dogs of the yard pace
for the stars and what they might do.
Inside, the debutantes sweat
under a ceiling fan
the maids failed to dust.
Across the hall,
in a studio pad of candles and Pez dispensers,
the TV rushes through commercials.
A few experts are on.
One in a blazer–
the kind with thick suede elbow patches–
calls the season a run-in with the laws
of bubbling tempers.
Still, hired hands spit coated seeds on the lawn
clapping at the falling of statues.
Barely anyone wants to panic
at the motorcycle flipped on its side,

leaking its vitals down the block.
Elite figures continue to deliberate.
Who else but them to stabilize unrest
and pander to slow-moving trains?
Very few of sound mind turn the stoves on.
And that's a fabulous good thing.
Lover, there is blood on the hydrants.
They see it. Oh, they see it.
It may have been the damp paint all along.
Indeed, the one we made
to match the lake–the lake that leads
to orange sunsets and smells of fruit
and what's forgotten. Just ask around.
And shake no one's hand
until you are safe aboard the ferry.
Renting space in a cold weather town.

Morning After a Protest

Returning home, the destruction apparent.
It's never been this bad before,
and there were quite some occasions prior.
Drains along the curbs burping old leaves
and fast food trash.
This disregard atypical of night.
At dark...horses don't chew through gates.
At dark...guardians rarely speak in codes.
Street lamps undress,
letting the potholes fill themselves—
these larger than life trees,
playing witness like hollow concerts.
Barely anyone walks outside today.
The litter is permanent nonetheless.
Whenever a storm brings more
than what is expected,
shutters snap close,
never seeing which flowers are brave.
But someone gently steps—
curiosity's pitter patter
hoping to stumble upon something untouched,

unphased by the upheaval around.
When they find a minted ally,
discernment says trap her under glass.
Then stare at her the whole voyage
while the ark takes them home.
Hallucinating and full of gin.
Drunk off commotion.
Whatever allows the kids to be fangless panthers.

Ichabod Crane
(Traveling)

I'm reading Marquez's speech on nuclear warfare,
and I'm wondering if this is the day,
a day when it happens, an event for moms and dads
to crouch over their young knowing they'll cough
white dust and expire.
What goes through your unwary brain
before the bright impact?
London rebuilt itself.
The girls in Birmingham had been in Sunday school.
Imagine seeing your own head on the broken ground
asking you why the rubble makes poster art.
You keep walking headless
until a stranger invites you in.
They talk to you without reservation
as you help yourself to half of a danish.
Neither of you are thinking,
there's no lamenting over falling plates.
It's the first time you've walked on cobblestone
and cracked knuckles with home bodies.
Everything is delicious,
the way you once thought it would be.

These Five

Rhode Island.
New Mexico.
Indiana.
Washington.
Alaska.
I'm staring at a poster of state flags.
Tacked to the wall nearest the side of the bed
where no one sleeps. Ranking all fifty up close.
Dissecting color, design and history.
Imagining them sway from capital buildings.
Interviewing natives of these territories.
Wondering which has low suicide rates.
The likelihood that women leave porch lights on
for their drunken beaus.
Thirty-somethings' assessments of the health care.
Recalling what first comes to mind at a state's name.
Attempting to boycott the lure of aesthetics
such replicas elicit multiple gazes.
The restless attempts in the wake of fresh walls.
Leading nowhere but to an orchard of pleasure.
A real smile made of nylon, just in time to start the day.
Using up my vacation time.

Daydreaming about going and not coming back.
Excelsior.

Election Year

The butcher dips his bagel in hot cocoa
while slouching in a diner that's barely out of the red.
From the peeling window a thin smoke
rises from an outside vent–the uneven street slick
with something that can't be rain. Oil?
Excess vinegar that tumbled off a shelf and
just so stained FMLA documents?
Three men ooze in, seating themselves.
One of them opens more sugar packets than need be,
the other–losing to his own spring jacket–looks through
everyone, the third can't keep still like trout
caught in a dripping net.
"This is the day the Lord hath made,"
says the regular woman
with the mole between her nose and light mustache.
Chatter–splintered declarations and lies–hits the ceiling
with broom handles, eggs sizzling from a kitchen
meant to be on display, capturing the seniority of
ripe banana-colored walls which haven't chipped
under the huskiness of pictures, laying the barrier
for the dizzy fish and his maritime comrades.
The radio stopped talking long ago, or at least since

the soldier and broker left screws on the floor.
It would be just the right scene for native sons
to return home, but the wind is not muscular and
everyone washes their hands.
Some mayors drill shamrocks into roads
while far off kings build matte dams and
rewind editors' notes. Except the teenager working 10-2,
no one knows the bacon is pre-cooked,
more eggs crack and hiss, popping behind
the horse thunder of steel feet bending the Mayor's curbs.
The trout leaps out of lemon water
as the call comes in—his son got accepted to an HBCU.
It's up to him now to blaze trails...shun donuts...
choke corruption.
"There is an opportunity for interstates of gold!"
shouts the lady.
That raisin on her face is growing a sprig of hair.
Will anyone service the flood in the bathroom
any time soon? After all, a girl scouts chapter
booked the off room for later.
"Shut the hell up," the linoleum yells back at the lady.
No one listens. But outside, a man lies on the ground,
bleeding from his shaved skull and the power company
can't fix the broken traffic light.
The waffles are remarkable.
There is no blood on the butcher's apron.
The royal guard...the mayor's police chew on rainbows.
Yeah, they swallow.
Check, please.

October

Walking over the leaves
is dwelling among a thousand stories.
The biting air undecided
on where it will overstay its welcome.
In that exact moment,
a few apples wiggle off stems
and roll in the wind,
I am left to choose.
So I stay until
the very last leaf spins
violently out of control,
granting me patience.
Then I walk home.
Ready for it all,
still hugging that orchard.
The kids on my heart the whole way.

As Seen on TV

They told me to shut up,
and bounce the ball...
Dribble...dribble...dribble...pop!
But I still have air left.
They told me to do my job,
so I caught the rock...
Juked...jump cut...hurdled...scored!
But I didn't dance,
we can't have all that.
It's about respecting the arena.
Sprained an ankle,
Doc looked me over as the news blared.
Making millions,
molding trillions.
I stand, they shout.
I kneel, they pout.
To hell with all this.
I'm running fast the way they like me to.
Won't slow down one pinch
until I blast through Capitol's thick door.
They're waiting on my black ass.
Bang...boom...pow...out!

Blood in my mouth,
signed poster in hand. Gone.
The TV at the doctor's office
showed it was cool.
Run boy...run...
straight to an ambitious end.
No air left. None. Gone.
But the TV people walk out and grab lunch
wearing my away jersey,
proud as when I entered the league.
Back when I was full of entertainment,
fast as all lightning.
Just the way they liked me.
Mum.
The way they lauded us.
Next.

Silence Culture (My Crappy Attempt at a Haiku)

The machine once said,
"I'm more than just convenience."
Then it was turned off.

PART 2

The Street with Flickering Lights

Rockwell Calendar

My ex-wife told me to drop our kids off at her mother's.
She lives in a house behind a factory that I
never see employees
come in or out of. It's not like it's vacant or
hurting for business, I believe.
When the oldest was an infant, I'd go out and
watch the stacks blow smoke high in the air. It looked
like the sky forgot to tie its belt around its wide waist
and something remained hanging. There has to be
a boss, either understanding or cold-hearted
with a mug on a desk. The inventory of this place.
It's a new era, but they've either went digital and sleek
on the inside, or everything's jammed
with paper and delay. My one daughter lowers the
window in the back. Unless I do the same,
that irritating sound will find my ears.
The last time I yelled things
got electric, and there were signatures involved.
To think I barely care if the curtains are shut or
parted nowadays! The last time those people came
I ate right in front of the window.
A heaping bowl of cereal with not much

milk for the effect.
They think I'm in my pajamas past eleven.
When I go to the store, they don't know I take
broccoli with brown strands, and leave the lovely stalks
for others. We stop for ice cream–
I use some of this month's rent.
My youngest doesn't talk, only licks her cone
and is the first to buckle into her seat.
I'm well with this scene, so much in fact,
I'm tempted to drive with closed eyelids just to see
where we'll stop–a country club for geese, a spot other
leased cars sit by the river, The Hamburg Fairgrounds,
or that lot with yellow lines where some
kiddos play hockey. My son's been asleep mostly,
but he carries the night bag without prompts.
Their grandma whips up some favorites,
and all is piping hot. I'm allowed to use the bathroom—
it's off to the side, and while in there
I take off my shoes just so my toes can knead
the rug and its microfiber caterpillars.
There's this Rockwell calendar tacked
to the back of the door. Behind by two months,
pictured is the one with the kid next to the cop
in the soda parlor. I take the nail out as the pages
fall to the floor without creasing.
My quiet one can be heard, asking for a napkin to
cleanup leftover sprinkles.
The old lady gave them ice cream. I mean...
she really did it like there's no tomorrow.
I kiss the ones I made, and even those in speculation.

'Til next week is our saying. All the car doors are open.
This is the last week I operate it.
It's going to take us somewhere grand,
neat and bubbly. Instead of watching porn,
I'm going to apply for a gig in that mysterious factory.
I'm going to get in there, and see what's
really transpiring. I can't feel the nail sticking the
pimple on my thigh, only that it's there.
I want to see someone enter and come out.
Pajamas or ill-fitting suit.
Doesn't matter.

Wednesday's Delivery

When I'm all loaded up,
and ready to blast out,
that's usually when they tell us there's express mail.
I'm instructed to drop those off first,
even if it's out of my way
and far from logical.
I grabbed today's box, irked and tripping on plastic straps.
The girl who hides her long blond hair
let me know it wasn't an ordinary one—
for I looked to read what said CREMATED REMAINS.
The piece of me where blood doesn't travel felt
an oozing shame for handling it without much care.
From then on, I could barely concentrate on traffic,
yet more so on the strips of tape and a stranger's attempt
at neat handwriting. What kind of life did so and so lead?
Did he or she know great streams to find trout?
If the goner had a choice, would it always be cookies
with dried fruit? I hit potholes the size of fallen stars,
and it didn't budge. No, not an inch.
I arrived at the house—the gray one missing shutters,
and used two hands to carry it, something I never do.
The relative wasn't even there to receive what was left.

I got it there well before noon, a job complete.
That's what a life has come to.

80's Kid

The giddy feeling all over,
late at night as *Weird Science* came on HBO.
There wasn't much I could do
to keep the TV from glowing,
huddled under the blankets on the floor.
Volume down. Remote in my hand.
Back then, they told you what to anticipate,
so as not to miss your chance.
I waited for Lisa to burst into their room,
my living room if dreams had pulses.
Not even aware of what my body could do.
But their creation laid the cement.
"Get to the part where she shows her tits!"
Out of that smoky green bulb machine,
leaning in the doorway.
Alas, those perfect lips greeted me
as a shadow fractured the bright frame.
My mom shook her head,
said she was disappointed, yet left me to myself.
And since then, I've been a man.

Returning Home at Dusk

A thick darkness with pockets of orange
stretches across the breezeway.
It was thrown together, rushed and taped
to the main rib of the house.
A torn ceiling open in parts,
for rain to disappear and darken the slats just above
where the banana seat bike sits angled up
against the chipping paint.
When I walk barefoot to get the mail
I know the wooden stalactites
will eventually repay me with splinters.
The downstairs neighbor swears there are
rats waiting to take us over.
She says so nervously with a long cigarette
and heavy turtleneck on.
When she shows me holes in the tile, I nod my head.
That is more so for the potential of this place, or better yet,
us being elsewhere in a greenhouse made entirely of
mint plastic where we sink our hands in soil
and wait to feel little nibbles,
all but turning in the keys immediately,

totally closed off to whatever could be explained.
The moon is out by now.

A Name

unique.
common.
burdensome.
drenched in nepotism.
some tumble off the tongue.
others—impulsive syllables
pushed down feeding tubes.
entertaining to read the ones
almanacs said were the talk one hundred years ago.
pets and infants traded courses
somewhere along the hike.
urging a young brown momma
to consider her child's future.
judged.
put in a box.
esteemed.
strangers wonder if there is meaning.
just to ignore its scrapbook and pasted quotes.
relatives whisper and grin
by the bedside of that mother exhausted by labor,
the squiggly hairs across her wet forehead.
a lofty trouble.

wishful effort.
years from now,
they'll ask what was left behind
more so than who left it.

Roswell (For Chris)

On my day off I visit you
in a brick building where most don't come home.
I sit at the side of the bed–one that resembles a 7
caved in–and watch the rise and fall of your chest.
Tubes and tape, thick wires and a perfect window
view spanning our city. Why can't I reduce myself and
hold your sweaty hand? It's not like it's mandatory for me
to keep talking, yet the beeping and hissing of these
machines make me want to unplug everything and
take you to the food court so we can talk about
women and risks. This room doesn't smell like mortality
or even warm juice. It takes on the empty odor of a
banquet hall days before a convention.
You're falling asleep as if to signal silence has a shelf life.
I want to doze off, too, dismissing the condensation
left by etiquette. The nurse knows we are not at home;
she knows I can barely look at your room.
She doesn't know I kissed your clammy forehead and
told you that I love you. We are men.
We reside elsewhere, miles away from April 1st.
I keep talking. And talking. Not rambling.
Over the machines between us.

Halloween Party '88

Mom applied thin coats,
but I wanted her to throw it on thick.
The white paint on my round chocolate face.
That year, I was Count Dracula headed to Cody's party
in his basement, cape tightly fastened, white dress shirt
missing the bottom button and pants
I usually wore to church. What a weekend dandy.
Mostly everything went together,
especially the plastic fangs—they jabbed into my gums and
left little room for talking. Who cares, right?
I was there to sell it until the end.
I put them in a napkin while I bobbed for apples
in freezing water, and when the pizza arrived,
I ate slice after slice after slice...
swept through a dish of candy corn.
Cody's mom complimented me
after my makeup rubbed off save for the blood
on the right side of my mouth.
Earlier, I used Mom's lipstick for an effect,
the original dribbles expanded then migrated
without anywhere to settle except down
my starchy collar. Later, my mother asked me

about it all. Didn't embarrass you, I replied.
She smiled wider than my fake teeth allowed,
never looking up from mincing garlic
on the cutting board. I took all of it off in
my bedroom. The costume. The posters.
The whole era of being seen.
Then I laid in my father's coffin,
just long enough to thank that tidy basement.

Fuhrman Blvd. Detour

It's a cloud dominant evening in early April.
Not too cold, but I won't be swimming or burning franks.
I run over the slick bridge and I hear them
before I see them—
seagulls jittery and grayish.
I've never seen so many at one time,
in one place and so deafening.
One group flies up as another hovers low.
They have a practiced system of sorts.
If I didn't know better, I'd say someone controls them
all from a string, only tightening the reins
when they almost touch the water.
A few stand on top of railing barriers,
long enough for me to think I have a chance.
I speed up and extend my arms.
They fly off the rusty pole and over the emerald water
just as others take their places.
Embarrassed to a degree, I scan the harbor,
but no one sees the birds taunting me,
certainly not the man far off walking on the other side.
A few minutes go by, when I pass on the right.
I apologize for I may have startled the gentleman.

Before I cross over, I look back and those water rats
are behaving like dons, squawking to a Friday song.
When I receive my wings, not if but when,
I'll let them touch me before
I take everything with me deep beneath,
the only trace being voluntary bubbles.
I'll give them a true show off,
a real dynamite show.

Saint Paul Said (Ye of Wholesome Faith)

Cursing under its spearmint breath,
brandishing some see through pistol
for all to measure and shutter at.
It's easier to admire its stride
on an even street with level spigots.
There may come a time
when all maybes and daydreams are shook
in a bag and rolled onto the floor,
yet downstairs it will remain about
eggs being scrambled,
bacon being thick,
flowers being trimmed at just the right angle
and all the villagers—with their theories and pacifiers—
gathered in the living room,
swallowing without aptly chewing
like it's their last meal in a copper town.

Wright and the Soap Man (For Henrietta Leonard)

I had the day off, physically.
But my mind worked that whole morning.
With nowhere urgent to go,
the kids and I ended up touring a mansion on a whim.
A Frank Lloyd Wright design
for this rich guy haunted by his youth.
The slide show before the tour said
Wright and this man often battled
over money, the architect's lavish visions.
Poor Martin just wanted to reunite his family.
It's what drove him over the years.
Not that brick building full of soap crosstown.
Restored Japanese art and family pictures,
particularly Martin's wife in the garden
and one of his boys lost in a thick book.
All these replicas carefully stretched or hung
along rather smooth walls and sleek aptitude,
telling stories, but leaving out those of the carpenters.
We walked along the pergola—that vantage point

of surveying bulbs and shrubs from an elevated view.
I recalled impersonating Martin—how it must've felt
to blow snow from the ledge,
the chorus of insects singing to horseshoes
lifting and falling. The air much cleaner back then.
Wright went on to write a book.
He came to his friend for help.
Once a self-made millionaire, Martin threw up his hands.
Everything worth bragging about lost in 1929.
What kind of look came over Wright's face?
Disbelief? Furrowed brows?
Still glowing at the magic of his own ruler.
One man all about freeing up space,
the other wanting to shorten its gaps.
I thought about the contrasts as I peered
through the smoke-tinted windows of the carriage house—
plastic fruit in a wooden bowl atop the counter.
I knew the door was locked, but I jiggled the knob anyway.
The builders and servants long since dust.
The gardener. His chauffeur. Their families, too.
I tried to assign features to their shapeless faces
during the walk to the exit and driving home.
I wondered if Martin was truly happy,
living in Wright's dear opus.
He achieved his boyhood dream.
He won the industrial heart of John D. Larkin!
Delta joined him, alas!
I pulled into the driveway and let the kids go upstairs
long enough to stand and pretend I was Martin—
begonias and hydrangeas roamed my nose.

Horse drawn buggies skidded to a halt.
The kids asked what's for lunch.
Returned to work the next day,
knowing what it was like to live glamorously.
I had to see it, just had to before I could move.
The kerosene lamp going dim in the upper unit,
signaling another day down, and we were finally one.
And then I went inside,
imagined I was Wright,
down to the walking stick and dropping jaws.
Erased the memories,
the ones that gnawed with mice teeth.
Just like the earth tone carpets,
the tour guides wouldn't let us study.
Soap.
The only thing fit for that day's lunch.

A Single Strand

The guy I work beside cuts my hair
after our shifts on paydays.
He whips out two mirrors, in which I survey his efforts—
the rubbing alcohol like flames on the back of my neck.
I wait to get home then study it all in the bathroom mirror.
One willowy piece of gray lies among the sooty black.
Reach for it, roll it between two fingers,
compare it to the rest
on my head. No difference except its color.
We get our money. He cuts my hair again,
shoves both mirrors before me—one for the front,
the other scanning the rear. The strand is there
where I last left it. Not quite contagious, yet.
Him and I work our legs to a pulp.
We get what we're owed. I show up and sit down.
This time I should talk to him about what's happening.
See if he's using a similar looking glass,
if he's ok with the shape of things himself.
Nothing goes past the surface, though.
I pay then leave.
Same as usual.

Oreo

About three or four mornings a week,
I open the scratched metal door
not knowing he's in front of it.
A black and white cat with a clipped right ear.
The widow next door refers to him as Oreo,
and at first, I thought it was a joke
until the skinny guy, who thinks he lives on a farm,
next to me revealed the animal's pitiful bio.
Some lady addicted to pills and gin left him behind
after she tiptoed out of the neighborhood.
The people around here
makes sure he survives. They adore him!
But not enough to let him crash inside for good.
With pineapple soda pop eyes—
those type that startle a person carrying groceries at night—
an orphan licks his self along the brick ledge,
waiting for charity.
I've laid out whole milk a few times
and some wafers that bear his namesake.
Kids lie and say he ate them,
yet I know what's really going on.
Rumor has it,

she's got her life together and has a new cat.
I wonder if our dear Oreo knows.
I wonder if he's aware of his own yawning in the sun,
wasting his afternoons on us, the androgynous reapers
begging like our loyal friend.

A Boss

"Chemistry between boys and girls.
It's a lot like when we went to the
woods and laid with the squirrels."
-Andre Benjamin, *Babylon*

It's like school was a made up brick storm.
Summer is all over our nicked knees.
We survive on fruit and weak breezes.
They won't let us venture far–
the probing voices, the distant voices of our mothers
that fire out our names, annoying these lazy afternoons.
The big girl–the forceful one the same age as you,
who rarely shows her bare legs, dares us to do it
in the clubhouse. It's more like a back porch
with space under its unpainted stairs, but it's ours
and we can curse in peace.
You go first, you're older than me, I say.
Your clammy hand goes down into my underwear
while sucking your other thumb.
The boss motions me into service.
Drag a finger across your waist, fumble over the lace
of yours like a chocolate wrapper, then travel down.

It's somewhere. Keep coursing. I feel the mounting heat.
There it is. Rest my hand. Let it stay while I look away
to find the coy sun. Boss girl stands by the trap door,
shifting between smirk and blank gaze,
snapping that rubber band under the nub of ponytail.
Go all the way, she requests.
The tiniest sounds make us jump, yet that fat thumb
with barely a nail, remains shoved between your lips.
Voices...faint...intermediate...splintered.
The crickets slowing to a murmur count somewhat.
All the voices factor in. Our moms call for our siblings,
though we only concentrate on two names.
My name, your name. Right under their noses.
Far...far...far away.
"We'll be there," we shout without saying nothing.
Just hold on, big people. Just you hold on, steadily.
We're coming home. Like we always do.
Way before the street lights tempt us.
Even dare us.
A shift complete.

Memalust (Timber)

Memalust (Timber)
I came to that fork in the department store
where I could stare at strangers or listen
to a song beginning to end.
Some indie rock band filled the ceiling
with hazy riffs and dreamy waves.
The lead guy sang about northern stars and
being trustworthy.
My wet bulky boots tapped the floor to the drum kick,
though the front man never repeated himself.
I had no way to find out the song!
No chorus. Bridge. Reverb lather.
If anyone besides me came away bothered
by such ambiguity they sure as hell tucked it in.
"I heard these guys left each other in the woods,"
some dude half my age strolling by with a girl said.
Hurriedly typed in: *Band who broke up in forest*
Nothing. Regroup. Think. Wipe phone screen.
Typed in: *Band who broke up in woods*
Again nada. Zilch.
Put my name and yours in. Hit search.
The whole store bellowed, "Memalust."

And so that's what I call the band
who makes no more music.

Buffalo Bills (For Christina G.)

If you're stuck go somewhere different.
Get out of your comfort zone, I was told by someone with
emeralds for eyes. So here I am sitting in my car inside this
windswept park. No one raked the leaves from fall,
but the soccer nets were taken down. Occasional walkers
bundled up, their breath hitting the cold air
while I scribble a few words then scratch
and make x's through them.
I drove here to take in a rare winter,
a whiteless one in this insecure town—
a town named after a lazy mammal's alias.
Take it all in she said, and that's purely what I'm doing.
The groundskeepers re-sodding the broken field.
I hear laughter rising from the soil.
There's a hope in the driveways and magic uncorked
at the grocery store. Just wish someone would
tell me what's so special going on in this place—
a place where I just can't get comfortable,
even once all the green returns.
Yet those eyes make me want to dance.
Those eyes...make me kick my feet up and shout...

Better yet, cause me to travel.
And that is a feeling, an action long overdue.
With or without their blessing.

Nothing

I typed your name in and pressed *ENTER*.
Nothing came up,
except strangers who shared the name.
My excitement fizzed
at an obituary,
but it belonged to someone in Kentucky.
I'll continue to listen to your baby sister—
your estate planner,
the one who tells fibs by the warm stove.
It's nothing.

Dishes

I walk diagonally, flick on the lights
and find myself in the kitchen.
A two-sided sink is filled right and left.
Crumb studded plates,
plastic cups and shining bowls
touched with cinnamon.
What's leftover swims in water—
now cold, yet frothy.
I wash dishes once a week.
Where I'm at, inside the melting cube,
that's overachieving.

-

The Regimen

I start and end my day the same:
with a pee.
The kind where I'm glad everything works
and I don't have to lean on a wall.
Sometimes yolk yellow,
sometimes clear like shattering ice.
Often blood orange if I think about it all.
They tell me to come out
and enjoy the randomness of the night.
"Throw back a few," they suggest with sour breath.
But real friends know I don't drink.
It could interrupt the colors,
it could have me breaking precious keepsakes
or mixing up my norms.
My days are my days.
Don't take that from me.
Please don't.

Nights in a Cube

Curves.
Curves.
Winding curves.
No straight lines.
Bending roads.
Uncovered suspension bridges.
Drinking water in my own house,
and all the guns are pointed at me.
Out the window,
green hedges ablaze.
A streak of ice disappears to the rug.
I pretend to go after it,
jealous of those lean fireflies.
They're outside.
They're action.
Breaking rules and glowing.
All night.
On my watch.

Tim Crews

It's a biblical miracle
I haven't snapped an ankle
on these uneven sidewalks.
I take notice of my socks—
the striped pair management can't dispute over.
The whole neighborhood at ease
with wearing extra pounds
of last year's leaves. Soon,
the new batch will cover the ground and
the muscles bordering my eyes will weaken
from making out too many shades of orange.
If it hadn't been for the mid-morning sun
licking my scuffed shoes, I would've
stepped on Tim Crews and kept going.
A Topps card featuring an LA Dodgers pitcher
who wore a crowbar mustache and hooked smile.
Didn't know kids these days still collect or trade,
yet there Crews was tucked under a dry leaf,
semi-bent, probably the result of him floating
from someone's high attic.
I take the card up, flip it over
skim the stats on the back.

Burlington...Stockton...El Paso...Albuquerque
to list a few—his best years coming as a true major!
I wish I could say his fastball was demented.
His slider wicked and reliable.
Those cleats with flaps over the tongues
kicking up the powdery mound
like a dog after it's been outside.
Yet I know nothing of this flameout
from Central Florida, only that he makes me
recall my less responsible days
when I traded cards and slid them
in leather albums. Makes me want to search
the No. 1 song on Billboard at the time of his peak.
Just who was jamming at large, then?
I should call up my best friend at that time.
We haven't spoken in many years.
Last I heard, he was madly in love
with a Connecticut girl who made him discard
his collection and focus more on the fine print.
It might not be the case now.
No hard evidence, really—just a dull feeling.
Of me—one maundering over raised concrete
stirring up the leaves.
Mixing an old sensation.
Protected by clear plastic.
An ace back then.

While They Slept

After making a racket all day
the world, or at least the part with influence, sleeps.
The journalist or transcriber or mere writer
or whatever sinks deep into the couch,
bites his split bottom lip,
waits for the last pin to drop,
for the snoring to get quite rhythmic and burly,
for the moon to say its quarterly prayers
before he begins.
Turns on all the appliances—blender, floor fans
and wind-up toys.
Considers yelling as high as he can,
flipping the light switch on and off.
They drove him to all of this—
those razor teeth piranhas chewing
through the bubble wrap.
He desired just a little quiet,
enough to gather and season his thoughts,
yet it rarely takes place.
They sleep peacefully like all the bills are paid
while he roars, hoping to shake them
long before daylight knocks.

Ideally, he wanted to write
during the day.
When his brain has vinegar,
when mostly everything works.
Is that too much to ask?
This upside down life he's chosen.
Among loud inconsiderate people.
Who sleep in socks.
Happily.

At Night

I should go to bed!
But this world protected by vinyl siding
won't let me fade away.
Closing my burning eyes,
hearing a determined river meet me head on.
But it's just heat rumbling from the vent.
I'm not getting much accomplished anyway,
so it's best I unzip what's cotton,
tucking in the bulk of human emotion.
I want to feel something
before I quit on the night.
No, I yearn to reinvent an impulse
only children at fairs can justify.
I'm looking to plunge down beneath
the waters I was told dreamers could only float upon.
I assumed I'd sleep well
after a hard day's work,
but my heart is still sprinting,
rummaging through what was said
and the wooden bishops before me.
All of it being anything except
weightless and soft to the touch.

I seldom recharge in this tackle box
of stray wires. The feeling of aimlessness
like telegrams from a distant planet.
I'm not getting much shut eye tonight.
And if I do? The next day will be
baby blue and hopeful, kind of promising.
No one opens the newspaper,
orange juice beside them,
skimming for pretty couples whose remotes
have fresh batteries and pantries lead to long life.
That's more of an afternoon sip.
I'm normally in bed by then.

Lazy Morning in July

A husky pocket of wind stops at my window this morning.
I can hear the garbage men yelling at confused cars.
My ex keeps bitching about how I need central air
whenever she drops the mail off,
and if not for the clock giving clarity,
I'd bet dusk is a priority
judging from the sky and its coffee bean clouds.
I should get up and shut the window,
that same wooden space I'll have to dry later,
but I only make it on to my elbow
before wiping the sweat off my ribs,
then back down in my own wet spot.
There's so much to accomplish today.
That job. A stop at the cleaners.
Batteries from the dollar store.
The book club invite I plan on turning down.
I'm the kick starter of dawn, usually.
Not today; I lie sprawled in bright undies.
Nothing to give the rain.
I'm already sucked through a straw.
Can't help but be late
for auctions I lack passion.

My chiropractor says such an attitude
is adequately lengthening the spine.

Dying Alone

Sugar water drips from a clear shrinking bag,
the chorus of doors opening
and chairs scuffing the floors
long since polished.
What would today give
to avoid a pencil and its thick foiled eraser?
As night shines onward
with little sign of regret
under its porch,
a man calls himself loved,
not for the evidence of medals
swaying in the divided wind,
but because they mention him in even tones
and wail at the ineptitude of language
for such dark times.
If anything gives out,
let its historians be supple
and reluctant in defense of legacies.
A will is fool's paper,
and air assumes deity.

What It Used To Be
(For Chris)

Jim Norton calls me Hollywood,
and the fact I have on green sunglasses
doesn't help my case, plus I don't
wear a shirt. I look for bright sneakers
and switch the factory laces for colors
I'd caution against on job interviews.
We don't run through the west side
enough, an observation I've long since
folded lengthwise. We're usually chasing
bodies of water, bending about risky
traffic circles slick with gas. I never
point out how the gas gives off
that spilled rainbow effect. I keep it
to myself and wonder about what
exact rubies the guys and I miss
when we're determined and
lovers of just asphalt. It's probable
there's a beautiful bird I miss
in the trees. I can't say I've seen
all the coffee houses or limping
cupcake shops. I'm willing to

accept these mornings look
immensely different from rooftops,
yet we dart down
these tight streets, curse freely
and pretend these runs won't end.
Somehow our legs find Prospect Ave.
I'm up ahead by now.
What used to be the Baptist church
bearing the street's name
now reads: Evergreen Commons.
Those waffle heads, smug in their
conquests, did it! Turned our past
into a collection of lofts, yet kept
it all the same, down to the steps
where that drunk whose last name
was Irish would bite his callouses
and wait for us, even in the bitter snow.
A cook at a soup kitchen in Allentown
told me ole Irish ran his mouth
to the wrong cop and got his skull
cracked–left him for dead.
I imagine where the piano once was
is now someone's dark film lab,
that corner we debated married men
while those whose eyes were glazed
over just stared through our buckles
and Windsor knots. The basement
set up with fold out chairs and
buttered brioche right before service.
Elio's gnarled fingers plucking

his guitar–our botched attempt
at painting the study one dripping
August. Where Pastor Jose told us
black magic and ballet can't intermingle.
Back to the slanted stairs where the
pretty mezzo-sopranos got into cars
and left without us each week.
At least the new regime didn't remove
the trees on either side, the shaggy ones
which cut the moon into eggshell pieces
when looking up. I ran past the wood
and brick like it wasn't there,
a gentle breeze in a windstorm.
Couldn't take off my sunglasses, or
grab the chunky door handles out front.
I could've ran a lap around the place
and still caught up. Didn't matter.
I couldn't cry with glasses that
matched the trees waving about.
Not by anyone who thinks
I've made it by showboating.
Not for all I thought we'd continue
to go through together.
On the west side
like I'd never ventured until then.

Quotes From the D-Boys

"Man, I don't trust them Arabs...
I made sure the landlord was the same
color as my skin before I moved in, dead ass..."
(A loud car rumbles over craters.)
"All I got is 25's on me...Come back in a half!"
"Yeah, bruh...I'm getting this bread. But shit, mailman,
I'm trying to be like you–
you getting that automatic federal coin.
Y'all hiring?"
(A new car rumbles over craters.)
"I got 25's, twin. You good? That'll work? Aight...
Hold tight."
(He fumbles through hedges and emerges.)
"All day every day. That's how we get it over here.
I report to me!"
(The shivering trees listen on the quiet block.)
"Yo, I told you all I got is 25's.
When you coming back, fam?
I missed my bus, but this cold little
Puerto Rican broad about
to pick me up. Straight like that."

(Cars stop and rumble on.)

Dion's Memorial

On the occasions I drive by,
I tend to find new articles each time—
the stuffed teddy bears
his loved ones try to keep filth off and
empty liquor bottles
clinking upside the telephone pole.
A collage taped across the wood yet
some entries are blotted
and curled, a circumstance of rain,
mist and petty snow.
There's one picture of the deceased from
his boyhood—a kid in drooping pajamas
with a whole day planned out in his eyes.
He probably ran up to the corner store and came back
on a friend's handlebars, only to run inside and grab a ball
and then back out for the court up the street.
Before all this, he told the girl, who wore ankle socks
and sass, that he read all the required books
from the summer list as she stood looking down
from her carpeted porch.
Years later...When the firing squad commenced,
some wave took him back to Lee's *Mockingbird*

and the humid jungles of Kipling's pen.
They shot into the gas tank
and left a hunched man up front.
I still smell fumes every now and then.
That is, when I'm not fixed on the artificial flowers,
when I'm not counting candles.
They left crosses on a street reverends don't visit.
I'm trying to note which gas is which, the fresh stuff
or just what lingers. But this is all just folklore they tell me.
It's a scavenger hunt; someone is truly dead–
all made up jazz, really.

Clean

Hasn't rained for weeks in this town.
That means no one calls me over to mow their lawns.
When I do, long showers follow, and I run
my pruney hands the length of my legs, yet still feel it.
The bits of heat-ravaged grass, dust and shredded receipts
in the hair of my shins and forearms.
Cleaning my short fingernails with my teeth,
pulling at my split ends to see how much hair
parachutes to the floor. Get dressed, put on mounds
of nautical sage deodorant. Heart set on smelling good
under this Canadian tuxedo I wear
to run important errands
like staring too long by the tabloid rack.
Rinse the day's troubles. Exfoliate the dry patches
where I lied and actually believed it.
Manicured. Soaked. And shaven.
Ready for bed. Clean, my dear.
In flowing cotton pajamas.
Still scratching and itching. Not tired.

A Filter

A mediocre display of true photography.
Straightened. Cut. Adjusted. And off center.
The manufactured shine.
So ungodlike.
Yet dazzling upon scrolling.
The doctored images are what will be kept.
Those are the beautiful ones
that convince us they really fell into our laps.
Really spoke about the world
and how it cranks out unrehearsed wonder.
The magnificence of thine options.
No blemishes to the untrained eye.
Continuously jealous
if all but a lifetime
as muted bulbs glow
like eyes in the forest.
Cropped.
Rather well-received.
A shield over what really happened.
Without one culprit.

Mary in the Glass

The giants stalked him,
left his face and arms rather swollen.
They weren't really giants or fallen angels,
just bigger kids who wouldn't let up.
When they took his bicycle,
that's the summer he stopped admiring her—
Mary encased in glass
under a yellow light atop the brick church.
There were even nights
on the way home from the baseball diamond
when he talked to her and asked for simple things:
the sharpness to return to an ailing mind, or
snow only coming the week of Christmas or
peace stretching 'cross the countries with long names.
During the day,
he imagined she slept and took few calls,
and woke up during rush hour traffic,
that buttery sheen glowing around her shoulders.
No tree branches tickled her fortress,
and the parishioners never let her come down
to draw on the sidewalks
or feel a raw November wind.

The boy eventually became a sir
doing what's instructed–sturdy employment,
babies and golf.
He moved far away
completely forgetting about Mary
and the parkway of supplications.
Yellow light. Green metal. Straight steeple.
A giant yanked him back to town–a ripe
plot of land, the prime rib of locations.
Never mind the last few hours
of a loved one who requested his face
one last time.
Doctors in his new town nagged
about cholesterol so he borrowed a bike
to see the listing.
If it moved him so, an offer would be made
the very next day.
No helmet to unfasten,
he got off and checked the address he'd written twice,
the moon winked overhead through the window
and bent out the other side in white squares
along the grass.
Our Lady of the Rosary Something Something.
A dull contrast between daylight and self-denial.
Mary didn't wave either hand; she shrunk
in his mind like a candle too relaxed.
Tomorrow, he'd take the land
and all its amenities: the contents of
an angled roof, whatever ceramic ladies
he cared not to embarrass,

and triangular light that split the ride home.
Such a place being wherever
they called him sir
on a bike under the moon,
the tall people long gone.

The Items

Inasmuch as I insisted
whatever items could wait until tomorrow,
the car pool would have none of it.
How did I end up in a grocery store
with them of all peeling crayons?
Carver politely ordered smoked ham,
gathered the couple behind us feigned glee—
something about a thorn patch unrevealed
to the common eye.
He pushed the cart long enough for me
to find Marquez whose sorcery in his veins
convinced the sample lady her demo oatmeal
was the mere hardening of panther tears.
The crowd alongside us balked initially,
the same which came along more and more
as the Colombian stopped smiling.
No one told us we weren't there as consumers.
For if it fit inside the cart with one wobbly wheel
then the item came with us—scotch tape, paper clips,
birch beer and Granny Smiths.
Without scuffing the heel of a man,
who used the calculator on his phone,

we turned down a quiet aisle where we found
the most famous Hemingway of all
on the floor leaning against cereal boxes,
bayonet in one hand and purple 3x5 memo pad
in the other. Eventually catching up, he flicked
a nickel towards a boy then passed me some tattered sheet.
The floors are yellow is all it said.
In those days, one didn't have to wait eternities
at the checkout, yet Dahl, being a smidge bored,
stretched his gangly arms, made menacing gestures
and ghoulish faces–the soldier ahead of us
being quite oblivious. "Something to pass the war away,"
he chuckled with an owl wink.
"Did you see that?" Baldwin asked everyone.
I, myself embarrassed by him pointing at me
and then himself. "The way that cashier looked
through you and I as though the lotto machine
is a more dignified stakeholder?
I would be more at ease in a strange land
without marked entrance or exit!"
By the time it all soaked in,
each one's quotes, shimmies and charm,
I sat on the couch alone
with peppermint tea and every item,
except the one I left home for.
An evening road trip with five dead guys,
and I never felt more alive,
the zest a dwarf harnesses
on a pin cushion of guidance.
That's when I heard the door open.

A thirsty mob that foamed for timelessness
wanted dinner and its collective patience had waned.
In my place. My meager space.
Stocked with some of the things I need.

A Helping Hand

If I didn't step just right,
I'd go straight through their raggedy porch,
so I kept my eyes down
and pretended I had no name.
The faint chirp got me to turn around;
it wasn't difficult to tell what it was.
Somehow a sparrow lied stuck in a rat trap.
Not the coiled square hammer kind,
but the plastic tray of bright green goo,
something like a sea of jello made to deceive.
I don't think I'd ever been that close
to an actual breathing bird,
the ends of its feathers sharp and fluttering
as I pulled it off or tried to.
Its curled feet stayed attached,
the legs had to be broken, I thought.
Legs like skinny helical screws
bent at a point and wings convulsing
at the prospect of flight.
I grabbed its body the way one does
when reaching for a cupcake with pretty frosting,
each time more of its coat left behind.

Death needed to come from human hands
rather than watching a morning turn into black.
I pulled as hard as I could
until it flopped onto the concrete,
stunned by its own disability.
Hopped. Tumbled. Plunged.
Down into the grass under a car
missing both license plates.
Desperate spasms took it nowhere.
I wish I could say I knew it lived on.
I can't say it made it back into the air.
That glass dagger it used to be parting the clouds.
Almost certain I did more damage than remedy.
I tried. Was delicate, careful as allowed.
I wanted to make things fanciful.
For that bird. And the people asleep inside.
Yet all I could do was hum...whistle...continue
down the street, its fight pulling me on course.
The feeling of finally helping,
a mood of walking tall.

PART 3

That Time We Painted Love in Your Nail Polish

Spiders and Oatmeal

She said life with me is like walking into a spider web.
Long after it's been pulled apart,
a nagging tickle lingers on the skin.
Can perhaps drive someone to paranoia—
madness, but that's debatable.
I'm listening to her conclusion,
watching rays of steam come from my bowl of oatmeal.
On she goes, comparing me to other forces—
hurricanes, abandoned silos, dead words.
Later, she'll pinpoint all that I'm not.
This is quality time.
We chew through our delicious meals of choice.
Her voice rising,
pulling the morning with it,
comfortable in my nest.

Sleep On My Heart

It hadn't dawned on me,
but we've listened to the album straight through.
I missed *I Sleep On My Heart*,
that's the tune I wanted to sing
as you play the drums on my back.
Instead, your fingers walk down my spine
before they reach towards the sweating glass on the stand.
The album plays through again,
a trademark of that navy night.
I want to rise and play you that song,
yet this is better.
You and me,
the smell of your hair locked in my pillows.
At least until the morning
when I remember all the lyrics,
and they mean something.
By then, you've been gone
longer than I care to admit.
While I slept on my side.

No Time For Love

I'd tell any green kid worth his syrup
don't collect much. Like stuff.
He'll become married to it
and bogged down.
It'll just make him stand at the microwave
when he's not hungry.
He'll pick up a Sunday shift
and fill his lady with cursive excuses.
Photo albums won't be kind;
he's a stranger.
The cousins a guy tolerates are laughing
and truly enjoying grandma's last stand
while he uses his pointer finger,
drawing figures across the backyard air.
He has the makings of a working man.
I've heard stories about such broncos,
and how they pick up houses
with the toasters still plugged in and children in bed,
looking for tight alleys to invade.
It's the rising and plummeting of numbers
keeping him awake. Not the calico by his side.
Nor the woman who whimpers at the bed's foot.

Crossword Puzzle

We use the same odd adjective "frazzled."
This has to be fate—pure homogenized pre middle age love.
When it ends,
that'll be the adjective stamped on our file.
The snow and sand still by our groins.

Purple Clouds in Outer Space

Astronomers dismiss it as an episode of fabrication,
yet I once made love to a girl on another planet.
Well...sort of kind of.
It was a *Home & Gardens* makeshift planetarium.
Her parents pasted stars and light blue moons
on the walls of the spare room.
The raised decals glowed in the dark, and as she slid down
my body I stared at the open ceiling past the glass and into
the cellulite of shifting clouds.
In a house filled with scratching animals and magnets,
the coolness of the sheets was enough to soothe
my dry elbows from the thick rug underneath our pallet
made for campfires and thin green tents.
She loved me.
I could tell from the way she stuffed
the pillow into the case and smoothed out
the tiniest of wrinkles before she handed it to me.
Lift up, she said in the dark.
She managed to put her hair in a bun
without me noticing, and for a few seconds I
substituted cows for dogs, whichever sailed over

the wire fence behind the house and returned
with muddy paws and the stick I'd thrown.
"Don't let me sully these white folks' sheets,"
my skin said to me. Was she breathing still?
She stopped talking, and all the groans I wanted to hoot
melted onto the rug and dripped away.
In the morning, she'd leave
for the Dominican Republic–
an ambitious opportunity to study abroad,
a librarian-to-be with nickel in place of sensibility.
It was the clouds, yes, the clouds
that impeded my concentration.
Thumbtacks of rain pelted the clear ceiling,
but the purple of the night kept me.
Inasmuch what the clouds made visible.
When I reminisce,
I'm not bothered by her wedding the man after me,
or the knots left in silk ties, as are the toiletries of war.
I am reminded when she arrived in sneakers
and brought home a rain/snow mix the week of
Thanksgiving, we kissed in the airport and talked
with our arms. Above the baggage claim there
stretched a ceiling solid and closed.
I needed to see straight through and give that nebula
an honorable name.
That's what comes to me,
riding these aluminum stars.

5:09 AM

A red vintage alarm clock sits wide-legged
on the night stand you let me have.
I never set it.
It knows heavy things.
Like things before they become "the thing."
The trendy breweries in the village,
the IPA's scooting down your throat,
the jeans you'll pick out
once you return to your college weight,
the dream job,
the perfect baby name,
and wide driveway your sister can't complain about.
Oh, and him—the industrial romantic
with hammers and passports.
It's a little past 5 AM.
I have to get up and lift heavy things.
But the clock doesn't know that type of stuff.

Blue Chair

Mid-modern style.
Midnight blue. Sleek in the light,
resembling something a superhero
would sit in after a long day,
and the uniform is on the hanger.
That chair, the one where I feel
like James Bond. The fanciest
piece of wood, upholstery and
cushion. The one in front of
the cheap curtains that blow
by the vent during winter.
Remember when you and I
and your dad drove twenty-something
miles to pick it up? I had to
bid on the frigging thing!
The woman who sold it
showed up to the door, a baby on
her narrow hip, more so happy
to be rid of me than the item.
Sandwiched between you two—
when I wasn't looking in the flatbed,
my eyes followed the veins of ice

that dribbled sideways across the windshield.
Heard about the chicklets
that nibbled on their own feathers in the coop
at your family's abandoned farm.
How the milk of your youth
poured out like white silk.
Or that time a classmate died
of congestive heart failure in a YMCA parking lot.
These days, the piece I almost missed
out on shrieks over the floor
when I move it to sweep.
It retains an odor of bacon,
characteristic of mornings–the same two-tone
mornings when I can't fake good posture
or will myself to drive.
Yet today, I undo the blinds. Take them off completely.
Look straight out the naked window–
the puttering cars, delivery trucks and walkers
moving to no universal scale, a broken orchestra.
This lemon sunrise darkens to amber, then night.
A splendid day and its wholeness gone by,
all from my sitting post.
The same chair we rode to get on black ice.
The one I swear leaves me the more
I half listen.

Honor System

I wake up to a crook in my neck
and her turning wildly onto NY-78.
Good thing I'm up in time
because there's a waltzing hornet
across the dashboard and I told her
I'm allergic, though I'm not.
She says her left knee is giving her fits.
A hint for me to take the wheel when it's clear.
It'll just be until the pain dies out, she says.
I reach for the pair of shades in the cup holder,
blow my breath over them and clean one lens at a time,
using the shirt a person I'm not allowed to
speak of bought. The windows are down,
and even when we roll them up
to talk about what occurred,
the sun bleeds through the panels,
highlighting the dust. My uncle always explains it
as an unforeseen misstep in judgement.
Yeah, that's what he told me to say
and let the rest seep out the window.
I'm not sure it's working, yet I do what he said
until we come to a stop. A dip on the side of the road.

No vendor. Or state trooper nestled behind the trees.
Just a shabby wagon hunkered down—a sign that reads:
JAM STAND $3 HONOR SYSTEM.
APPLES NEXT WEEK.
Of course we slow down and get out.
The beady eyes of squirrels and critters
too small to make out playing hosts.
Peach butter. Blueberry Pomegranate. Cherry Preserves.
She takes a mason jar up to her button nose. Twists the lid.
Inhales deeply like it's a handful of delicious joy
fresh to the world. Behind us, pickup trucks hissing by.
At a speed that suggests they'd kill me if there was no law.
She's content. It's a real smile. Her gums exposed.
Her cheeks holding what's left of summer.
I stuff two balled up dollars in the lockbox.
The rest she covers in change. She says we'll stop
for plastic spoons at the first gas station we find.
I stay tight on the invisible shoulder closest to traffic.
She shoos me off. The lady keeps driving!
What a damn warrior.
Far from where we came. Nearer to the epicenter.
I plan on coming back next week.
Alone. For the apples.
A question or two for my father's brother
when I buzz him. I'll drive over his way.
We'll enjoy some oranges.
If this ride ever concludes.

The Drive

We went to a pristine nook of a town famous for ice.
She said we needed to chat
about our marriage and the sour spots
that someone else licked.
She's driving, like really gripping the wheel,
owning the winding curves while I'm trying
not to fall asleep with playdough in my hand.
I'm dozing in and out,
fighting past the serious knocks to the ribs.
She's talking about a kid who lived across the street
when we come to a white church—
the kind you see atop a hill sketched on a calendar.
It's ski country smack dab in summer, very few tourists,
even the bridge we rattle over is less stressed,
somewhat forgiving. As the sun tucks away,
it reminds me of an apricot
that some machine, much bigger than me, is chewing.
She keeps on with nostalgic blurbs,
excited about whatever's ahead, this smooshed in town
I've never been to.
I really want to make a grand display of this clay.
Really mold it to where we can talk and peel layers.

I can't fall asleep. She's driving.
Owning some of it.

A Warm Bath

I've brought home pizza from your favorite place.
It's one of only two ways I show I love you.
You're listening to AM radio,
some song about sand and horny Egyptians.
When I enter the living room,
you only turn up the volume and pretend to read.
Remember that one time, the summer it barely rained,
when we went to see the all-black people circus?
Yes, it poured on the way to the car
and your hair reminded me of wet cotton candy.
I drove and you drank the whole way back.
When we arrived,
our driveway didn't seem so crumbled and slanted,
my key with the dirty yellow tab fit the lock,
and I tossed you on the dolphin print couch,
which used to be your grandma's.
Before the past due gas bills and overgrown milkweed,
we would sit cross-legged with board games
and play them upside down
until the sky does that wonderful transition
where clouds are animal crackers and ivory stars stare
back like cat eyes.

You're not drunk tonight.
You ask me to join you in the water upstairs.
A nice hot bath,
anchored by four lion paws
and a ledge great for holding incense.
We can get it back, you say,
nibbling by my collarbone and rubbing
where I usually keep a wallet.
For whatever reason I didn't hear it,
but you've been running the tub before I arrived.
Maybe it was Pharaoh's music,
or the buttons of your romper making a sound
as it faints off your thighs and hits the first step leading up.
I plan to meet you for our own warm bath,
I'll do so fully clothed.
We're way past bathing as a resolution,
I just wanted to hear the faucet's roar
produce enough blooming force
to turn the magazine's pages.
The article is still on the same page,
and I've been back for a lifetime already.
There's dinner waiting under the chandelier
when we're done.
I love you today.
I've easily done right,
manning our lighthouse of wax
and ushering in what counts.
The pizza's getting cold, darling.
It's from your favorite place.

Wind Chimes

She invited him over
for lemon kimboucha and critical thinking.
He wants to come inside,
so she keeps him on the porch,
sandwiched between hanging plants
and a wicker table–
an old gnome and short stack of books on top.
She's talking as he rearranges the books
by width and length in his mind.
Even her pet iguana bothers him less
than when they were a buzz.
To be rocking in chairs
like it's a painting of a farmhouse
is quite something considering it's the city.
It's in his back pocket–the thick bronze coin
they used to flip for tough decisions.
And as if all the unruly opinions
could giftwrap blank dimensions
for the sake of a hush, they rise
to touch the wind chime at the same moment,
a dull chorus lassoed to the sunset.
They stare into the street,

and then at each other,
and then back out into the griddle of still cars.
He runs his hand across the pocket.
It's the perfect shape of a house,
minus windows and a satellite.
Her fingers want to pinch for the coin.
But they tap the small metal poles again
while the other hand holds his
and her heel stops the door.
Some kind of summer music–
half of it could go either way.
The ringing...
The touching...
The circling back to one.

Violet Submarine

Somehow I've managed to salvage this creation
with duct tape on its starboard fin.
Off come my clothes and down
the tiny snorkel hole I fit.
Seldom does anyone ride along
and when they're allowed, it's just so
I can do tricks 'round the coral reefs
and lecture about fresh water
or how biology is unfair.
Zipping through the ocean,
I'm reaching at stunning artifacts—
jewels winking on the murky floor
and hired divers whose only language is rising bubbles.
Yet I can't touch them.
The thick windows get in the way to a fault.
My transportation of choice and design
wards off enemies, lowering its yellow beams
as not to startle the fish.
And like a father, who doesn't plan on staying,
I am gone without explanation or promise
once the school rushes the hull.
I'm surprised those company sharks

have not bit into my periscope, yet—
a cautious mariner bracing for the month
when premiums soar.
In this submarine,
I am a king who doesn't raise his voice
nor threaten with foam tridents.
I am as content on dry land
as I am in the company of hammerheads
or the pressurized graves of rusted ships.
Occupying this cockpit,
I laugh at my jokes,
sing off-key and navigate as though
Gatsby made it out of the pool.
But the truth is:
I'm in the bathtub
under old water.
You're tapping on the door,
saying something about a curling iron and kiss,
but no rush.
I pull the round plug from the drain and start over.
Mermaids exist,
two-seaters,
fog protection,
pruney fingers pressing random buttons.
Something along those lines...
No rush.
I slap the water,
applauding a patience not my own.
Then you barge in.

The Night Shift

I'd be your nagging hangnail if you let me. Just to be a part of you and the glee you emit like slanted light bruising a stained glass window. Our once electric union now reduced to a whisper in the guest room filled with open music boxes and refurbished snow globes. Oh, lover come back to me if indeed this sea can reach a calm, a relaxation we only theorized, some tulip field we couldn't trample if we dared. Every night, or most of them, when the world decides that sleep is trendy, and it's done looting my fossil fuels, I smell your DNA everywhere. My eyes rapidly blink until the sun yawns; it never says good morning or anything worth printing on a t-shirt, but rather reiterates a supposed fact. Allegedly, I never cross your mind, and that's a pill, though crushed and pulverized, I still can't swallow awake. Good night.

Snowy Park

Early on a January Sunday, I rose to run through a park
with a dead garden.
Faded sheets of memories were the same grey
as the snow that barreled
out of the clouds and onto the cracked blacktop.
Around a bend, two cardinals
clenched to a twig encased in pure ice
reminded me of a magazine
promoting maple syrup. It all seemed bleached–
from the middle-aged walkers
to the bare trees atop the hill where kids sled.
My nose frozen with crust on the inside.
I couldn't see lillipads anywhere
beneath the pond's lazy mist.
It was the wind that made everything quit and
rolled berries to the sewer vent, but not all the way down.
I threw the spare key into the gray pond.
Yet before that, I slipped and fell.
Maybe it was truly my fault.
Still, I kissed all that moved then went home–
my own cheap cozy one-man
icy jukebox. I don't know exactly how many miles I ran.

Or if I even put one sneaker in front of the other.

Tulip Bed

Every spring, when the tulips poke up out front,
may you think of me.
Yes...even after you've shoved the very last brick
from the house into your backpack,
and the airplane is on schedule.
The others can't live.
The neighborhood cats loved craftsmanship.
They left messages most mornings
and ignored NO TRESPASSING signs.
I'll die believing those little bastards can read.

East Aurora in Spring

I swore I'd never venture back,
though here I am,
bumping into the five & dimes
like left and right elbows.
Even the air smells out of my price range,
and swollen birds know only bottled water.
Strolling these even sidewalks,
stepping occasionally to peek into boutique windows—
the baristas decorated with unstained aprons,
spinning toys, hot fritters and pink cakes
almost squeeze me off course.
I am here to buy the perfect gift—
one that can only come about
by forgetting this little town
and all its beautiful pocket mirrors.

Farmer's Market (For Raymond Carver)

The car I leased worked perfectly well,
so I took the bus
just for some scenic diversion.
I ate a brownie
and stuck a clipped tulip between my knees.
The entire ride,
some teenager stared at me
when he wasn't fixing the tubing on his slingshot.
A crumpled transfer and smell of exhaust in my clothes,
the thought of jam took me to a muddy slab
of commotion across Bidwell Pkwy.
White Rastas blew on saxophones.
Political merchants sold felt kites
and smoked jerky in tents.
On a saw-tooth of grass the lifelong opera began.
I met a girl who sold blackberries in a hazmat
and untied duck boots. We married, had ingrates,
wrecked a house and shared a journal.
I already had someone at home
the day I shopped local.
It was the same day I gave up cursing.

I guarantee that teenager's rubber band snapped.
I'm almost sure of it.
And that fucking bitch
has yet to mend the plastic tips of those shoelaces.
We read each other's entries.

The Mailbox

Likened to a cardboard truce,
she called him over for what remained of a dozen.
Donuts. Some glazed. Others plump
with cream or the kind that look
like wheels with deep ridges.
Just while they searched for plastic
to store the sweets and memories,
a postcard blew off the mantle
and onto the rug by the door.
She laughed about the paint he spilled
that day she received keys to the place.
That was a time when mistakes were
just feathers on the scale
and the refugee, who collected bottles and cans
in a cart with a long pole attached,
wasn't a nuisance.
The postcard, one from Michigan,
wedged between the threshold and door's corner,
still looked the same as the day it arrived,
not one side worn.
On it, was a picture of two shirtless boys
holding walleye above their golden hairlines

in the sun—the hooks deep in the oozing gills.
Something tapped on the railing outside
as the man crouched after it.
It was him—the leaning man the neighborhood
knew as Gallagher.
That day, it wasn't a request for tin and rummaging.
Ole Gallagher took it out of a box—a vintage fan,
a matte green with sharp blades,
one you'd come across in a muggy tent in Vietnam
that spun regardless of breeze.
The hobo read off a name on the box,
connected the brand to a sweeter point in history.
He gave Gallagher a few bucks
and let him keep the fan for presentation.
On the short drive,
he ran his fingers over the bag,
traced the box's dimensions and remembered
two pieces of tape side by side.
One for her maiden name, the other somewhat peeled,
yet still aglow along the mailbox's lid.
Most of the postcards clipped
to a clothesline over the door
were addressed to him, and he didn't live there.
He mulled over such a thing
as he ate a piece of each donut and laughed
at the homeless man, who actually read
the brand name correctly.
Ole Gallagher really made no errors
during the spelling bee—immaculate pronunciation.
That tickled and tormented the man

well into the night.
His name grew more exotic a few houses over,
shopping cart wheels rattled
to the soundtrack of promises
down an avenue too narrow for do-overs.
He forgot to pick up his mail.

A Year's Muse

Knees deep in shreds of colored
construction paper on the linoleum.
Waiting for some saving rope
to appear and lift me towards the ceiling...
Every rattle makes me think
of our old toaster and your call to come
get breakfast.
Every 7-Eleven makes me remember
the slurpies we gave 3-star reviews
on the stoop by the highway.
Every poem I write I tear up,
rewrite it, bandage it with gauze
and make it rhyme for you.
Every field I walk through,
I talk to ugly weeds and ignore
the stunning lilies because...
we were never voted cool.
Every fight I recall, I strip it
down to its underwear and church socks
knowing the silence is a floating hatchet.
I've taken down pictures–the rhombus-shaped
ones and skinned the frames made from

sugar water and plaid ligaments
just to admire them in a box.
Flailing in a sea of torn pages.
Every successive breath gurgling over the top
in determined effort to find you.
By chance our paths split and burn...
Just everything, vitriol and applause,
was about you. And the fury to go on.
Everything. Perhaps all of it.
Submerged in your warmest qualities.
I took an intermission from scrapbooking
to let you know all this.
Distracted. With paper cuts. So off course.

To Sum It Up

I adored something
that didn't love me back
so I learned to prize
something that cherished me.
The space in between,
more so the duration it took
to arrive where I'm currently writing from,
saw wrecked Chevy's,
leaning Christmas trees,
flourless cupcakes
and beautiful views from bridges.
I'd do it all again,
even lie to myself
just to see this technicolor dream wave
sparkle beneath my feet
and melt the falling snow.
Cool.
Cold.
Warm internally.
Sometime.

A Text Message

Successful transmission.
It made its way soundly wrapped
in the colored tissue paper
of safety and good intention.
Yes, I received the text message.
I read it.
Reread it.
Attempted to erase it.
Cursed at it.
Never let my blood pressure soar.
Guessed how many drafts it underwent
before it traveled and landed as is.
I took it with me
to the crowded market,
down into the basement
with a ball of laundry.
It sat beside me
at dinner and made the pork chops
less alive.
For whatever reason,
I can't smoke its leaves
from a supine position in bed.

I've memorized it
down to the marrow
of structure and punctuation.
It sits fragile
like the blossoms of May.
Yes...I received it
without hindrance.
Dabbed its congratulatory
raw batter on my freckled tongue.
I'll reopen it once
the morning yawns.
I doubt I'll respond.
Rapture wins.

The Shower in Salamanca, NY

In a mid-tier hotel.
The skin I'm carrying actually feels pliable
just because I'm unemployed
and the phone is not ringing with favors.
Warm like an oven of empathy,
a shower head—the size of a sunflower—hangs
over me and gives its best rendition
of the tin man paying it forward.
Doesn't take much fiddling
for the temperature to find its groove
unlike tiny apartments the kids complained about,
the ones landlords raised rent
when a raggedy ass gig cut hours.
Those same upstairs swamps
our leaning furniture and cold cuts lived.
The water is warm. Dare I say...perfect.
But not too warm
as though thousands of ants march under my skin.
I close my eyes, stand tall
push back my crumbling shoulders
with my mouth a tad agape,

wet needles learning my chest.
I can't open my eyes,
or the dreams won't come true.
There's a mound of dirt by these toes.
The time I blew the mortgage.
That Saturday I talked too long.
When I forgot our anniversary.
I didn't pay for all the grapes.
And prayed with my eyes open.
Under the moon, feeling someone's bride.
Writing bad checks to boy scouts.
Learning swear words in another language.
Getting drunk, misquoting Martin Luther the King.
Introducing Jesus as my homeboy.
This water feels pleasant. Dare I say...therapeutic.
Not too soothing
where a man spills all his secrets.
I turn the knob sideways.
And wrap myself in a towel.
It's a miracle I don't knock anything expensive over—
the lights dim and eyelids tightly sealed.
Long enough to catch a chill,
I lean against the leather foot stool by the bed.
The phone rings, loudly.
I pay it no mind.
When I let a damp towel fall off of me.
That weekday I walk backwards,
turning the faucet back on.
How I let the cold water abuse me.
Not caring if the phone jumps all night,

or that I'm on the run
from anything lukewarm,
of anything totally sure.
Countless times I proclaim it:
this water is lovely and cold.
Downright frigid like I'm used to.
Icy. Blue. And familiar.
Strangely, the right degree.

Literature &
Hormones

Books. I keep many books on the bed.
Volumes. Editions. Reprints. Original covers.
I know I won't get to read them all.
But I sleep with them.
They say if you love something you'll sleep with it.
She and I haven't occupied the same bed.
They say that means it's real love.
This world follows no logical rubric.
I sleep with books,
and make love to her in my mind.
Anything more is a novel.
I'm just learning to write my name.
So...

Big Mother

At the ridge,
there's a beefy hill that can outdo the imagination,
an alpine maze opening up in stages.
I've seen some quality guys give out
before they make it to the halfway mark,
before acid shoots everywhere
and the hamstrings seize off the bone.
Been running curves, dips and grooves
of the park for years now,
admiring the way chimney smoke
is visible in the distance on a clear day.
Even thought I heard a bear rumbling
just before dark when I was alone one time.
Darted back to my car—sweat and funk
lathered all over me—and they were sitting in the grass.
He sat with a beer can near his foot
while she paced, a lit cigarette that dangled.
"Won't we just end it now if you have to be
so dramatic every time," he said.
The woman paused. Flexed and shifted her toes
like she put the cigarette out under her.
But it was still the same one in her hand.

He mostly drove the conversation
while she whispered, yet I couldn't make out her words.
Perhaps a middle schooler could see
the white flags in his pupils,
the surrender in the slurring voice.
"I'm done," was all he kept saying,
every so often twisting at the waist for the can.
If it pleased her, she was close enough
to kiss and kill him. I don't think they ever
noticed me, for one pulled at his own hair,
and the other rocked and sniffled,
then the pacing started once more.
Just what did that wrinkled woman smell?
Fresh tar by the entrance?
Court orders torn to pieces?
The abrupt finalities of spring?
The massive hill my running buddies and I
call Big Mother sat there waiting for them.
I wanted to suggest it,
though they'd probably made it up before.
The alcohol and mumbling at dusk
were nothing new.
Despite her never taking a drag,
I gathered there were cheaper hills to climb,
smaller ways to work up a sweat,
then retreat just before the stars bombarded
the course with more hypotheticals
and no ends in sight for miles on miles.
That torturous hill sparing no laymen,
stretched and available,

just beginning to warrant its name.

A Song

After all that happened,
they shared it.
Neither humming in the other's company,
but rather apart, at separate times
in different cities, yet the same one.
He at least owed her that.
A full selection.
No incomplete drum loop.
Real composition this time.

Full Lips (For Jennifer Harris)

A well-traveled relative
told me full lips hold twice as many words.
I've heard lips say things like:
"That sweater looks good on you!"
or
"Blueberries are good for memory."
or
"When I get out the car don't look at my butt."
Those that show up well on camera
dipped in gloss,
chapped by stray winters
stained in Tuesday night wine.
"It was a blast."
Lips that ask:
"Is this the right thing we're doing?"
When I think about it,
all I've known are thin lips–
tight former-smoker we got a long way to go lips.
"Sorry...I...just need to...take a step back."
Where can I find full lips?
The kind that match my kiss

and say a lot barely open.

Full lips.

Kiss all of me, please and thank you.

Walk Again (For Diana Vera)

Let's get lost
just to be rebellious.
My 9-5
is to make you feel loose.
It's winter.
Strawberries are out of season,
but I'll take you
to a field where that fruit
will eventually call home.
Lying is ok today,
but not to each other.
Wear that sweater—
you know...the blue one...
with the tuba collar.
I'll pick you up at—
just be ready.
Love letters aren't me.
You unwrap my candy.
We're rolling like
a baby face boulder down Main St.
It's snowing a tad,

flakes melt over your curls.
The bakery,
where I had a break-up in,
whizzes by on your right side.
This city's a blur,
we're jazz over dinner.
What do you want to do?
Tell me which destination
is green tea at your laptop
and whole milk for your recipe.
It doesn't matter, you say.
The rise and soft fall
of your eyebrows signal
you really mean it today.
Think dumb poet.
Think fast, you broke dreamer.
Driving on sunshine
more so than 1/8 tank of gas.
Once you told me something—
a story from the papers.
A menace to women
who hid in thickets
and did bad things.
They found him, praise God.
Who would've suspected a doctor, a family man?
But his disciples are out there,
wearing no masks.
You haven't walked alone in months!
Think quick.
This could be it...

We end up in the woods,
one with names on its trees,
kicking pine cones,
searching for bluebirds,
our gloves left on the dash
like fools and children.
You don't bring up Jack the Ripper
or his copycats once.
Chubby clouds come out your mouth.
Your glow softens the meadow.
Just when I think we're done,
you ask me to snap a pic.
And for a second,
only your grin comes into focus.
I hand over my phone.
You're pleased with the photo.
The copycats by the trees
never catch your eye.
Remark after remark is about
what's light and falling.
The snowflakes–white constellations
you can touch and still live.
That's adventure.
We're not even cold.
We've only just begun.
I believe you'll walk again.

PART 4

And Then Came Children

Daddy Was a Quarterback

Through this hollow theater we travel.
We walk with shabby sticks, the fake conservationist types.
It's one of those days
when the sun couldn't make a mistake if it tries.
And we go without sunglasses
for fear we'll miss certain mysteries—
like husky shadows and the transfer of pollen.
I yell at the girl for not wearing boots,
usually the boy slips in mud.
If I had half the arm of Wilson,
I'd hit one or two of the deer
darting through the bushes and over the mossy logs
in the far. As if this cheap adventure were not duly
picturesque, we bump into a stream.
A weak current is just enough to amaze the children—
limestone rippling across before splashing
and sinking below. My good arm is tired,
so we continue to walk the way those in gift shops do.
All that is missing, perhaps a few sandwiches
and thermos to share. My good arm renews itself,
but the girl's legs need rest. She picks out tree stumps

before seeing the crumbling mushrooms
on the gaping bark. I crack a gnarled branch over my knee
and can't hear the stream from our seats.
To the boy I am strong.
He is embarrassed to pee on twigs.
If it weren't for the hopping starlings,
all motion would halt.
I should kiss them both.
I cannot leave this place.
Thor in joggers. The father of clear Sundays.

Karate Orientation

The studio accommodated us on a Sunday.
I like the master already.
Using his mother as protection,
my son—with warm blood in his cheeks—hides behind her.
Things like this cost money
and though we don't argue over such feathers,
unwritten rules stand firm.
I'm here to be a friend
to a boy who wants a real sword,
and his classmates to answer his phone calls,
to acknowledge him and faint lasers.
He'll feel like a gallant conqueror
once I doubt him, and he has little choice but to destroy.
Even me. Us. Them.

The Wind

"Dad, there are a lot left on the trees,
and it's already October," he realizes.
He wonders if all the leaves will swirl
to the grass before winter barges
back into our lives. I reckon the Lord
does things to keep us on schedule, I reply.
"Like what?" he asks, balancing an acorn
with his untied sneaker along the small hills
tucked beneath the uneven ridge. I almost start
to list examples—downpours emerging after two-week
droughts, viruses humbled to a rumor
once newborn snow caps waiting branches.
But it's the wind this morning.
Nameless. Thick. Surrounding us. Its strongest ally
being its own biting self. It's the wind that will do
God's work in perfect timing. One day he'll witness
that for himself—the surety fortifying his pace
and lungs that crave brisk air visible to the eye.
For now, a sheet of pink light coats the ridge.
We barely appreciate its effect on all it hits,
the raw beauty dressed over these leaves.
We're busy studying the ones yet to fall,

those needing coaxing for flight.
On this bald hill. Lovely pink glow.
Rather submissive.
Both of us maneuvering on the fly.

A Quick Dinner

One wants broccoli.
The other keeps me at the sink,
washing slightly crushed blueberries,
which stain my fingers.
It's one of those weeks
when the grime stays in the hem of my pants
and their bickering sucks on my bones.
I turn the stove on,
the faucet runs cold,
in the next room a finger-smudged flat screen
has no audience, so it takes a hurried nap.
After they leave forks and crumbs behind,
I may just ask to lean against the front railing
and crane my neck to take in the smell
of factory cheese and trampled candy.
I will ask them if it's okay. It's a permission thing.
I can't anger them. I've come too far.
They rule heavy-handed and sleep lightly.
These egg shells for walls have yet to inquire.
Finding the TV remote breaks down the ice.
They're so young and power hungry.
The children need to eat.

I, being their chef or someone they need.

Earthworms

The 7-year-old I'm responsible for
is fascinated by earthworms in spring.
I mean...What mound of curious testosterone
isn't at that age? One hand pulls apart the wet grass
like a scalp, the other calls me over to view a catch.
I want him to feel all of the planet
without a magnifying glass,
and get dirty save for the sweatpants
already patched in the knees.
On evenings, by myself, I pluck red bulbs
from budding trees and hurdle puddles.
Sometimes the worms make a lake of this water,
the blood and veins apparent in their squirming bodies.
I forgot to tell the kid I saw a robin–
the kind that looked as if a loaf of bread sat in its chest–
toy with a fleeing worm before he gulped it down
and hopped along the sidewalk the other day.
He will want me to describe every detail of the bird
so we can find it and talk specimens in a circle.
When I was his age, I never left the lawn.
I'd still be there if it weren't for the
maps held in their beaks–those bored robins pittering on.

Free to do whatever they wanted. On and off land.

Woodlawn Beach

Fried chicken, worn towels and cola.
Oh, and a story about the days
before each of us came to be.
That's all my grandfather needed
to pack us in the Impala and head for the beach.
This very day,
I'm sitting on a blanket loaded with sand
watching the kids and wife belly flop over waves.
Seagulls come right up to me
necking for scraps,
reminding me of that time when a rude one
made off with my brother's drumstick, and
another nabbed his biscuit while he chased the other.
I want to get up and stroll along the shore,
right up to the point where water
turns sand dark brown before rushing backwards.
Cross my legs, lean on one elbow,
stretch out to one side, attempt a prone position,
but the whipping fragments will have none of it.
Meanwhile, the kids are having a grand day
under the sun, ever so often coming back
to ask for the time, crunching down

on a cookie or potato chip.
I really should walk the beach.
I get as far as my knees
using my hand as a visor to see a boat far away,
a bobbing pyramid within the horizon.
No one makes me,
but I cut the water like a shark to surprise them.
Everyone caught off guard I joined in
just to be thrown by powerful water
and the burn in our nostrils.
I let everybody go out further,
simply so I can scan kite surfers
and odd body shapes tanning ashore.
I should get out,
at least to see what I'm missing.
I do so just to plop back on the blanket,
the sand somehow infiltrated our food and dry clothing.
All this time,
my grandfather couldn't swim a lick,
something my grandmother revealed many years later.
The way he carried me on his broad back
and tossed me within hairs of the sun.
The bravery involved to count, shuttle
and frolic with us all.
I don't recall him ever using a watch
or checking the blowing sand.
My grandmother might state otherwise.
But I really should take that walk.

Dad & Boys

So I'm sitting in the car,
and I come to this part in the book
where a boy farts in the backseat.
The main character is repulsed,
the stench making her reconsider becoming a stepmom.
At that very moment, I smell it!
My son does the very same behind me.
He normally shrugs or blames a sibling.
But today, just him and I, his eyes dart
east and west, and he fesses to it,
almost proud like he outsmarted cancer.
How ironic that the make-believe and factual
joined hands, not letting go.
I don't think it has ever happened
before in history—a man reading a scene
and it occurring before his very eyes.
In a car almost paid for, no less.
There I sat with all four windows down,
drops of rain finding my thigh,
the biological father of a trail blazer.
It all smelled of brilliance.
It marched without standing up.

From the backseat. From the backseat.
Exactly there.

Frosting

An hour and some change late,
but there was no rush.
Really there wasn't.
We picked up the birthday cake,
and she was certainly satisfied.
I tried to consider her tastes
for cartoon rainbows and pastel calligraphy,
and let her know it was me
who chose the colors and placement of everything.
An afternoon when we sat
at an unfinished table for a windy picnic
and walked the curving pier,
yet it was only me who walked super-fast.
The kids get it,
like they really hurry for nothing
and can tell if the folks aboard
the catamaran are having a good time
in the distance.
We stayed out almost until midnight.
I couldn't believe they didn't give out
in the backseat, so there I was
lighting candles and singing in the dark kitchen

to a girl dead set on getting a slice
with the thick frosted rose.
She got the pink one,
which if it were real would've received
dozens of gazers during a walk,
the way it opened up.
Her brother happily took the blue,
and the excess smeared from the knife
on to a paper plate
decorated with a border of flowers, of course.
Before I knew it, it was just me in the dark.
I ate a slice,
closed the box
and drank milk straight from the carton,
then repeated those steps again.
Someone cut on the lights,
asked me why I was staring
at the box atop the oven.
Couldn't tell which one,
sometimes their voices braid together.
The surgery should begin dead center
not on the arbitrary edge of a cake.
"Nothing, just tired," I said.
That's all I could come up with.
"Come on, let's go to bed. It was fun, right?"

His Jam on the Dial
(For Landry)

Friday morning
driving under a steel cloak of grey,
traces of the night before
still lingering with its dark posture.
"Can you turn it up?"
I can't get mad
seeing how he says please.
Didn't sleep well,
but the glow of cars' frog-eyed beams
wake me up in passing.
Listening for that youthful octave,
singing his song,
reciting those lyrics.
Before he gets out,
I turn it down a little
held by a tiny vocal embrace,
then back out the icy driveway
with enough to get by now.
The sun beginning to prick through
as I ooze into traffic,
already late for work.

That upbeat tune. Him. All worth it.

Boulevard Mall (For Megan Malone & Other Buffalo Kids)

On Saturdays, before the current gig squeezed my schedule, I'd take the kids there. I forgot about all the weekends I rode the carousel as a cub. Ma would buy us French fries from McDonald's if my brother pleaded long enough. Those skinny salty fries not like the fat crinkle-cut ones that stuck to the cookie sheet at home—the kind cut from fancy potatoes forcing our momma to deliver on a promise. One weekend (my brother probably doesn't recall this), another kid and his mother stood ahead of us. She let him get the large size, and he didn't have to share like us! I ate my portion slower than usual, so I could finish with the lad. Without having to whine or roll on the floor, he got to bounce on the merry-go-round—his smile probably not as wide as I'm making it out to be, yet it did soak up the light. Then it happened. Yes. He vomited starch and cotton candy all over the blank ponies and couldn't stop—a pink soup no amnesia could mop away. Ma packed us up and out we went through the rear exit, then lamented on the way home.

"I just feel bad about it all," she confided in the rear view. Bad? For the child? Her fellow mom?

Now I tell the kids, "Back in my day, you could eat or have fun." But not both. Certainly one or the other. That was when I had time. Before this damn job took my weekends. I have kids now.

A Day and Its Wonderful State

Today I was being.
Being worried.
Being scared.
Being indecisive.
Being giddy
only to come back down.
Being rushed.
Being told to slow down.
Being taught by unlikely teachers.
Being called names
not on my birth certificate.
Being praised.
Being vilified.
Being elsewhere.
Trying to be present.
Being a father.
Being their rolling stone.
Being myself.
The hardest of being.

Here's Space to Write a Poem. The Kids Thank You.

LaGuan Rodgers is a writer, father and distance runner born and raised in Buffalo, NY. *The Kids & I* collection comes on the heels of his debut book *While Waiting: The Musings of a Complicated Mailman*. Follow him on Instagram @lgtheroyal for more insight into his world and adventures. His essays can be found at: laguanrodgers.medium.com Hold on. Be strong.

Nicky So is a children's illustrator from Indonesia. The former psychology major states her biggest aim when designing is to try to place herself in the world within a child's mind and bring it to life for others to enjoy. *The Kids & I* is So's first contribution to a literary project. Find her vibrant work on Instagram @nickysoart for samples and artist updates.

CPSIA information can be obtained
at www.ICGtesting.com
Printed in the USA
FSHW020813270921
85003FS